Dear Parent:
Your child's love of reading starts here!

Every child learns to read in a different way and at his or her own speed. Some go back and forth between reading levels and read favorite books again and again. Others read through each level in order. You can help your young reader improve and become more confident by encouraging his or her own interests and abilities. From books your child reads with you to the first books he or she reads alone, there are I Can Read Books for every stage of reading:

SHARED READING
Basic language, word repetition, and whimsical illustrations, ideal for sharing with your emergent reader

BEGINNING READING
Short sentences, familiar words, and simple concepts for children eager to read on their own

READING WITH HELP
Engaging stories, longer sentences, and language play for developing readers

READING ALONE
Complex plots, challenging vocabulary, and high-interest topics for the independent reader

ADVANCED READING
Short paragraphs, chapters, and exciting themes for the perfect bridge to chapter books

I Can Read Books have introduced children to the joy of reading since 1957. Featuring award-winning authors and illustrators and a fabulous cast of beloved characters, I Can Read Books set the standard for beginning readers.

A lifetime of discovery begins with the magical words **"I Can Read!"**

*Visit www.icanread.com for information
on enriching your child's reading experience.*

For old skateboarding friends

Balzer + Bray is an imprint of HarperCollins Publishers.
I Can Read Book® is a trademark of HarperCollins Publishers.

Fox Is Late
Copyright © 2018 by Corey R. Tabor
All rights reserved. Manufactured in China.
No part of this book may be used or reproduced in any manner whatsoever without written permission except
in the case of brief quotations embodied in critical articles and reviews. For information address HarperCollins
Children's Books, a division of HarperCollins Publishers, 195 Broadway, New York, NY 10007.
www.icanread.com

Library of Congress Control Number: 2017951356
ISBN 978-0-06-239872-7 (trade bdg.) — ISBN 978-0-06-239871-0 (pbk.)

The artist used pencil, watercolor, and crayon, assembled digitally, to create the illustrations for this book.
Typography by Dana Fritts
Title hand lettering by Alexandra Snowdon
18 19 20 21 22   SCP   10 9 8 7 6 5 4 3 2 1
❖
First Edition

I Can Read!™

SHARED
My First
READING

FOX
Is
LATE

By Corey R. Tabor

BALZER + BRAY

An Imprint of HarperCollins*Publishers*

Fox is late.

Fox is late for lunch.

Go, Fox! Go!

Fox does a kick flip.

flip

Fox does a *big* kick flip.

Fox does a nose slide.

Fox does a *long* nose slide.

Go, Fox! Go!

Fox does this trick.

Fox does that trick.

Go, Fox! Go!

Fox goes over.

Fox goes under.

Go, Fox! Go!

Fox gets flowers.

Fox gets *lots* of flowers.

Fox gets food.

Fox gets *fast* food.

Go, Fox! Go!

Fox gets home just in time.

Stop, Fox! Stop!

"Oh, there you are," says Fox.

"Just in time for lunch!"